Field Trip!

Landfill

Angela Leeper

Heinemann Library
Chicago, Illinois

© 2004 Heinemann Library
a division of Reed Elsevier Inc.
Chicago, Illinois

Customer Service 888-454-2279
Visit our website at www.heinemannlibrary.com

Designed by Kim Kovalick, Heinemann Library; Page layout by Que-Net Media
Printed and bound in China by South China Printing Company Limited.
Photo research by Jill Birschbach

08 07 06 05 04
10 9 8 7 6 5 4 3 2 1

Library of Congress Cataloging-in-Publication Data
Leeper, Angela.
    Landfill / Angela Leeper.
        p. cm. – (Field trip!)
Includes index.
Summary: A simple introduction to the purpose and workings of a landfill, describing what happens to garbage after you throw it away.
    ISBN 1-4034-5162-1 (HC), 1-4034-5168-0 (Pbk.)
    1. Sanitary landfills–Juvenile literature. [1. Sanitary landfills. 2. Refuse and refuse disposal.] I. Title.
    TD795.7 .L436 2004
    628.4'4564–dc22

                                2003014524

Acknowledgments
The author and publishers are grateful to the following for permission to reproduce copyright material:
pp. 4, 6, 7 Robert Lifson/Heinemann Library; p. 5 John Hawkins/Frank Lane Picture Agency/Corbis; p. 8 Patrick Bennett/Corbis; pp. 9, 10, 11, 12, 13, 18, 20, 21, 23, back cover Jill Birschbach/Heinemann Library; p. 14 Tom & Dee Ann McCarthy/Corbis; p. 15 Chinch Gryniewicz/Ecoscene/Corbis; p. 16 John B. Boykin/Corbis; pp. 17, 19 Corbis

Cover photograph by John B. Boykin/Corbis

Special thanks to our advisory panel for their help in the preparation of this book:

Alice Bethke
Library Consultant
Palo Alto, California

Malena Bisanti-Wall
Media Specialist
American Heritage Academy
Canton, Georgia

Ellen Dolmetsch, MLS
Tower Hill School
Wilmington, Delaware

Special thanks to North Wake Solid Waste Management Facility and Butch Brandenburg and Onyx Glacier Ridge Landfill, Horicon, Wisconsin.

Contents

Some words are shown in bold, **like this.**
You can find them in the picture glossary on page 23.

Where Does Your Garbage Go?

When you throw away garbage, it goes to a landfill.

Landfills store people's garbage.

Landfills can be near or far from your neighborhood.

A landfill begins as a big hole in the ground.

What Kind of Garbage Goes in the Landfill?

Every day you make garbage.

You may throw away food wrappers and food scraps.

You may sweep the floor and throw away the garbage.

All of these things can go in landfills.

How Does the Garbage Get to the Landfill?

Garbage collectors pick up garbage from people's homes.

They drive the garbage to the landfill in a garbage truck.

Garbage collectors may not go to homes in the country.

People take their own garbage to the landfill.

What Happens to the Garbage at the Landfill?

Garbage comes out of the back of garbage trucks.

Trash compactors push the garbage into a pile.

Trash compactors make the garbage flat.

They drive back and forth over the garbage.

What Happens Next?

Trash compactors put dirt on the garbage.

Dirt helps keep the landfill safe.

Dirt keeps the garbage from blowing around.

It helps keep smells out, too!

Why Are There Birds at the Landfill?

There are many kinds of birds at the landfill.

Most of them are seagulls.

They are looking for food.

Can a Landfill Become Full?

Every day more garbage and dirt go on the landfill.

It becomes higher and higher.

After many years a landfill
becomes full.

It cannot hold any more garbage.

What Happens When the Landfill Is Full?

When a landfill is full, it looks like a big hill.

Many landfills become parks or even golf courses!

People still need a place to put their garbage.

A new landfill is made.

What Should Not Go in a Landfill?

Plastic, glass, metal, and paper should not go in a landfill.

All these things can be **recycled** and used again.

This big bin holds things that will be recycled.

This saves room in the landfill.

Landfill Map

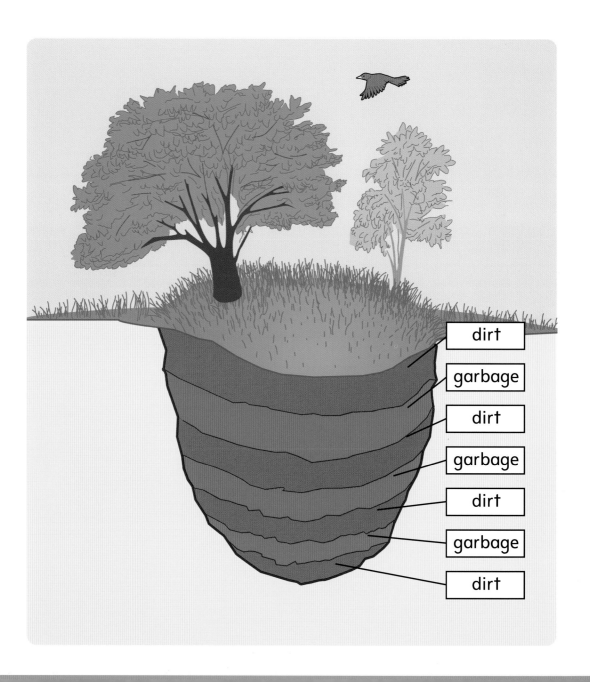

dirt

garbage

dirt

garbage

dirt

garbage

dirt

Picture Glossary

recycle
pages 20, 21
to use something again

trash compactor
pages 10, 11, 12
big truck that can push things

Note to Parents and Teachers

Reading for information is an important part of a child's literacy development. Learning begins with a question about something. Help children think of themselves as investigators and researchers by encouraging their questions about the world around them. Each chapter in this book begins with a question. Read the question together. Look at the pictures. Talk about what you think the answer might be. Then read the text to find out if your predictions were correct. Think of other questions you could ask about the topic, and discuss where you might find the answers. Assist children in using the picture glossary and the index to practice new vocabulary and research skills.

Index